IN A PUMPKIN SHELL

Over 20 Pumpkin Projects for Kids

by Jennifer Storey Gillis

Illustrated by
Patti Delmonté

ISBN 0-590-97527-7

Copyright © 1992 by Storey Communications, Inc.
All rights reserved. Published by Scholastic Inc., 555 Broadway, New York, NY 10012, by arrangement with Storey Communications, Inc. TRUMPET and the TRUMPET logo are registered trademarks of Scholastic Inc.

12 11 10 9 8 7 6 5 4 3 2 1   6 7 8 9/9 0 1/0

Printed in the U.S.A.

Recipes in this book were originally published in the following Garden Way Publishing publications: pages 46-48 from *Bread Book*, by Ellen Foscue Johnson; pages 52-53, *Maple Syrup Cookbook*, by Ken Haedrich; pages 40, 42, 50-51 from *The New Zucchini Cookbook*, by Nancy C. Ralston and Marynor Jordan; pages 35-36, 38-39, 44-45, 56 from *Winter Squash and Pumpkins*, by Mary Anna DuSablon. All titles are available through Storey Communications, Inc., Schoolhouse Road, Pownal, Vermont 05261 (1-800-827-8673).

Table of Contents

Be a Pumpkin Gardener   1

Make Your Own Pumpkin Patch   2

Care and Feeding of Your Pumpkin   4

How to Harvest and Store Your Pumpkins   6

Create Peculiar Pumpkins   9

Grow a Giant Pumpkin   10

Impossible Pumpkin Facts   13

Growing an Award-Winning Pumpkin   14

Saving Pumpkin Seeds   16

Be a Pumpkin Artist   17

Paint a Pumpkin Still Life   18

Pumpkin Pillow   20

Pumpkin Seed Necklace   22

Make a Musical Instrument   23

Pumpkin Painting   24

Make Your Own Fall Foliage Centerpiece   26

Make Your Own Jack-o'-Lantern   28

Pumpkin Lore   31

Puzzling Pumpkins   32

Be a Pumpkin Cook 33

Good Kitchen Tips 34

Pumpkin Soup 35

Pumpkin Tureen 36

Fried Pumpkin Flowers 38

Pumpkin Waffles 40

Pumpkins Afloat 41

Pumpkin Snack Chips 42

Pumpkin Pie 44

Pumpkin Rolls 46

A Bonny Bowl 49

Raisin-Pumpkin Cookies 50

Maple-Pumpkin Cookies 52

Pumpkin Seeds 54

Pumpkin Bread 56

Pumpkin Butter 57

Crossword Puzzle 58

PART I

Be a Pumpkin Gardener

It's that time of year again! Grown-ups are
pulling on their green gloves and rolling out the
wheelbarrow — it's time to plant the garden!

You can join in the fun and success of the garden by
planting your own bumper crop of pumpkins.
Not only are pumpkins easy to grow, but what else could
you plant that would grow to such an enormous size and
have such a beautiful color?

Open the next few pages, and discover the
wonderful world of pumpkins!

Make Your Own Pumpkin Patch

WHAT DO I NEED TO GROW A PUMPKIN

- Enough garden space to plant seeds 4 to 6 feet apart
- Pumpkin seeds
- Shovel
- Peat moss & dried manure
- Lots of water

Choosing the Right Seeds

- If you want a GIANT pumpkin — try Big Max seeds.

- If you want a pumpkin for pies — try Baby Pam.

- If you want yummy skinless seeds for eating — try Triple Treat.

- Or — try a few of each and see what you like the best!

1 Soak your seeds in lukewarm water overnight before planting.

2 Decide how many pumpkin plants you want to grow. Be careful — even one plant needs a lot of elbow room.

3 Dig one hole 2 feet deep and 2 feet across for each pumpkin. Fill the hole with soil, peat moss, and dried manure. This adds the nourishment the pumpkin needs in order to grow big. If you plant more than one, make the holes at least 4 to 6 feet away from each other so there's plenty of room for your pumpkins to GROW!

2

Put 3 or 4 seeds on top of the freshly dug soil, and push them in just until your fingernail is hidden (½ inch deep). Pat dirt over them. Water the seeds well — but not so much that they float away!

Take good care of your seeds after they sprout. They are baby pumpkins and need lots of attention so they can grow up strong! Water them well when the earth is dry. Pull up weeds that grow near them. Make sure they aren't shaded by other plants — they need 6 or 8 hours of sun shining right on them every day to grow their best.

TIPS FOR PLANTING PUMPKINS

★ **Don't** plant pumpkins near potatoes. The potatoes will suffer and there won't be mashed potatoes for Thanksgiving dinner!

★ **Do** plant a few pumpkins near your squash. You may create some "squumpkins" — a silly but special treat that sometimes grows when pumpkins and squash are planted near each other

★ **Do** plant near corn. The pumpkin vines will discourage raccoons from stealing your corn.

Care and Feeding of Your Pumpkin

Weed

Try to keep weeds away from your pumpkin plant. By pulling weeds out with your fingers, you will give your pumpkin more room to grow. Weeds use up the water, sunshine, and nourishment in the soil that pumpkins need for themselves.

After you have planted your pumpkin seeds, you need to pay attention to them all summer long. Here's what to do:

Water

Make sure to keep the soil wet. You may have to water your pumpkin every other day, unless it rains.

Mulch

Put a covering called *mulch* around the pumpkin vines. You can rake up the grass clippings after the lawn is mowed and use them for mulch. You can also use straw, leaves, or even seaweed, if you live near the ocean. Pile up the mulch about 2 to 3 inches deep, but leave a little space around the stem of the plants. When you use mulch you surround your pumpkin with lots of the nourishment it needs, and you also help keep the soil around the plants moist.

Prune

When your pumpkin vines begin to grow, flowers will bloom along the stems. Each one of these flowers will be a pumpkin when the time is right! If you cut off some of these flowers, the ones you leave will grow into bigger pumpkins. This is called pruning.

You may not want to take any of the flowers away, but just remember that the flowers you save will grow into bigger and stronger pumpkins. Choose the one flower on each vine that looks the biggest and healthiest. Snip off the others with your fingers.

How to Harvest and Store Your Pumpkins

How do you know when your pumpkins are ready? When your fingernail *can't* penetrate the skin of the pumpkin, then you can cut it from the vine. Don't worry — your pumpkins can't overripen on the vine. You can let them grow and grow until you want to pick them — just make sure you pick them before the first frost. Here's how to harvest your pumpkins.

If you want to store your pumpkins to use over winter, harvest them on a sunny day, when it hasn't rained for a few days, if possible.

Have your helper cut the pumpkins off the plant. Be sure to leave the stem on the pumpkins.

BLEACH SOLUTION

1 cup of chlorine bleach mixed with 1 gallon of water

Caution: Bleach solution is poisonous — use only with a grown-up helper!

Do not carry your pumpkins by the stems — they are not strong enough to support the weight of the pumpkins.

Try not to drop your pumpkins or bruise the skins — they won't keep as well and will spoil more quickly.

Wash your pumpkins with the bleach solution and sponge. When you get all the dirt off, the pumpkins will look nicer and you'll also protect them against germs that cause them to spoil.

Let your pumpkins drip dry. You don't have to worry about rinsing them off or drying them with a towel.

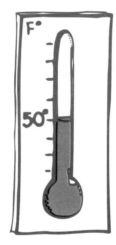

Cure your pumpkins by leaving them in a warm, well-ventilated spot (like a porch) for about ten days. Curing them dries and hardens their skin so that they will last longer.

Store your pumpkins in a cool, dry place that is about 50°F. Make sure the pumpkins are not touching each other. A cellar or attic where they are out of the way seems to work best.

Use your pumpkins all winter long! You worked hard to grow them — now enjoy them!

PILGRIMS' PUMPKINS

A member of the squash family, the pumpkin is a native American vegetable. Pumpkins were plentiful during the time of the Pilgrims, who had a little rhyme describing just how many pumpkins they had:

We have pumpkins at morning
And pumpkins at noon,
If it were not for pumpkins,
We would soon be undoon!

The Pilgrims made pumpkin beer out of persimmons, hops, maple sugar, and pumpkin.

Create Peculiar Pumpkins

Personalize Your Pumpkin

• • • WHAT YOU WILL NEED • • •

- Ballpoint pen
- Sharp knife
- Baby pumpkin

When your pumpkin is very small, write your name on its side with a ballpoint pen. Have your grown-up helper use a knife to go over the lines you made, so that the skin is broken. As your pumpkin grows, so will your name!

Create a Square Pumpkin

• • • WHAT YOU WILL NEED • • •

- Milk carton
- Baby pumpkin

When your pumpkin is very small, place it gently inside a ½-gallon milk carton. Be careful not to break it off from the plant — just ease the milk carton over the pumpkin. As your pumpkin grows, it will fill the shape of the carton. Your pumpkin will end up being square!

Grow a Giant Pumpkin

- Use Big Max seeds for best giant results.

- Start your seeds inside so you can get a head start on the season. (Outdoor planting shouldn't be done until you're *sure* the weather won't get frosty and kill the tender young plants.)

- Plant 2 or 3 seeds in a small container (such as a milk carton) about 6 or 8 weeks before you would plant pumpkins outdoors. You will probably want to plant seeds in 4 or 5 containers, so you have more than one plant to put in your garden.

- Once the seeds have sprouted, cut off all but the strongest plant in each container.

- Put the containers on a bright, sunny windowsill to grow. Be sure to keep your plants watered.

- When it's warm enough to plant the young pumpkins in the garden, put the containers outdoors every nice day for about a week and bring them in at night. Gardeners call this *hardening off*. It gets the plants gradually used to their new outdoor world.

- Select your planting place carefully. You need a spot with plenty of sunlight and plenty of room! If you plant more than one pumpkin seedling, plant them 25 feet apart.

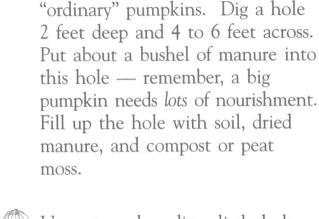 Prepare the growing spot even more carefully than you did for "ordinary" pumpkins. Dig a hole 2 feet deep and 4 to 6 feet across. Put about a bushel of manure into this hole — remember, a big pumpkin needs *lots* of nourishment. Fill up the hole with soil, dried manure, and compost or peat moss.

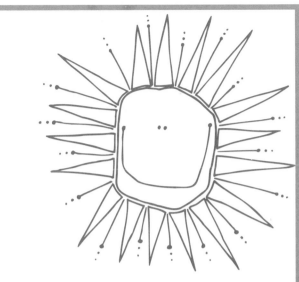

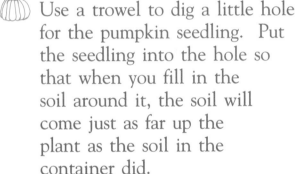 Use a trowel to dig a little hole for the pumpkin seedling. Put the seedling into the hole so that when you fill in the soil around it, the soil will come just as far up the plant as the soil in the container did.

Be sure to handle the little seedling very carefully so that you don't break it. Never hold it by the stem.

Pat the soil firmly around the plant. Water it well — but don't let the water hit it so hard that soil is washed away or the plant is damaged.

Pull up any weeds that grow nearby.

In late July, prune all but one flower from the vine. Protect this plant carefully from the wind and other garden foes (such as insects that chew the leaves or vines).

Keep a 2- to 3-inch layer of mulch around your plant.

Check your plant every day and give it lots of water whenever the soil begins to dry out.

Every 2 weeks, feed the plant with liquid fertilizer or MANURE TEA.

Stand back and watch your pumpkin grow!

MANURE TEA

Fill a 5-gallon pail one-quarter full of manure. Fill the pail to the top with water. Stir the mixture every day or so. After it has "brewed" for about 2 weeks, use it to nourish your plants.

Impossible Pumpkin Facts!

Wow! The Atlantic Giant pumpkin seed that was created in Nova Scotia *can* produce a pumpkin that weighs 400 pounds. The record-breaking weight of an Atlantic Giant is 821 pounds.

This is as much as a small cow, *and* . . .

it is enough
to make
400 pumpkin pies!!

Growing an Award-Winning Pumpkin

Many county fairs and grange fairs award prizes for vegetables — such as perfect pumpkins! Here are some tips to help you win a prize with a pumpkin you are proud of.

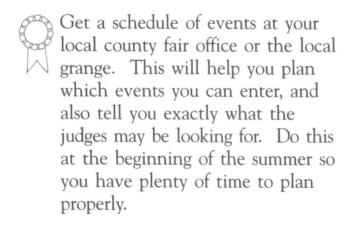 Get a schedule of events at your local county fair office or the local grange. This will help you plan which events you can enter, and also tell you exactly what the judges may be looking for. Do this at the beginning of the summer so you have plenty of time to plan properly.

Be sure to keep track of the kind of seeds (called *variety*) you plant — the judges will want to know.

 As your pumpkins begin to ripen, turn them carefully every few days so that they ripen evenly.

 Place a small wooden board under each pumpkin so that it's not resting on the ground. This will keep it from rotting.

 Choose your best-looking pumpkin to take to the fair. Remember — the biggest isn't always the best!

 Wait until the day of the fair to harvest your pumpkin. To have the freshest pumpkin, water the plant in the morning and then pick the pumpkin right before you leave for the fair. Leave 2 or 3 inches of stem on the pumpkin.

Wash your pumpkin with water and let it drip dry. (Do not give it a bleach-solution sponge bath.)

 Remember to carry your pumpkin carefully — not by the stem.

 Wrap your pumpkin in burlap, newspaper, or other covering, and pack it in a box in the car.

Good luck! Be a good sport — winning isn't everything. Walk around and enjoy looking at other people's hard work, too.

Saving Pumpkin Seeds

Here is a way to get a head start on next summer's crop.

•••WHAT YOU WILL NEED•••

▶ 1 pumpkin
▶ Sharp knife
  (and a grown-up helper)
▶ Bowl of cold water
▶ Plenty of paper towels
▶ Clean glass jar with lid

1 Choose a pumpkin that is completely ripe, and get your helper to cut it right down the middle.

2 Pull out the pumpkin-seed goop, and put the seeds into a bowl full of cold water. Separate the seeds from the strings. Wash the seeds until they are clean.

3 Spread the clean seeds out on layers of paper towel. Let them dry for a week. Turn and move them around at least once a day, so they don't sit in any puddles.

4 When the seeds are nice and dry, place them in the glass jar, and screw the lid on tightly. Label the jar "Pumpkin Seeds." Put the date on the label. Check after a few days. If you see any signs of moisture in the jar, spread the seeds out again to dry some more.

5 Put the jar in a safe place. At planting time next year, your seeds will be ready to use. They should grow up to look just like their parents!

PART II

Be a Pumpkin Artist

There's more to a pumpkin than meets the eye.
Not only do pumpkins make fantastic
jack-o'-lanterns for Halloween, but you can
decorate with them and design your
own garden art.

Harvest a few for your studio, roll up your sleeves,
throw on a smock, and let your imagination go wild,
as you peek at the following pages!

Paint a Pumpkin Still Life

WHAT YOU WILL NEED

- Old shirt or smock
- 2 tables
- Newspapers
- Paper (at least 12" x 18", if possible)
- Watercolor paints
- Paint brushes
- Glass of water for cleaning brushes
- Stack of books
- Pretty towel or sheet
- A few pumpkins of various sizes
- Leaves
- Candlestick with candle
- Basket
- Green bottle

1 Put on your smock and find a comfortable table where you can work. Cover the table top with newspapers, and set up your piece of paper, paints, brushes, and glass of water on the newspapers.

2 Find another table to arrange your still life on. Put it where you can see it clearly from your artist's chair.

Stack your books near the back of the table. Spread your towel or sheet over the books. Arrange the pumpkins, leaves, candle, basket, bottle, and anything else that you think is pretty. Sit in your artist's chair. Can you see a little bit of each object you arranged? It's okay if you can't see whole objects — in fact, it looks nice when they overlap some.

supposed to look *exactly* like the real thing. You have an artist's eye and should feel confident using it! Have fun!

Remember to clean up! Wash your brushes, recycle your newspapers, and put all props away.

Get comfortable and paint what you see.

Have a friend paint along next to you and then compare the differences between your paintings. It is not

Pumpkin Pillow

- Plain-colored fabric
- Scissors
- Fabric paint and paint brush
- Pins
- Large needle
- Yarn
- Pillow form or polyester fill

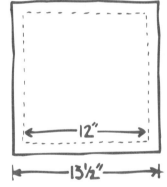

1 Cut 2 squares of fabric that are 1½" larger on each edge than your pillow form. (For example, if your pillow form is 12" square, cut fabric pieces 13½" x 13½".) If you use polyester fill, cut two identical pieces of fabric any size and shape you wish.

2 On one of the fabric pieces, paint a pumpkin! You might want to draw it with a pencil or chalk first, so you get it just the way you want it before you put paint on the fabric.

3 Let picture dry completely. Follow the directions on your fabric paint tube or bottle. Many paints must be ironed after they dry, so that the paint won't rub or wash off the fabric.

4 Take the piece of fabric that you didn't paint on and cover the painting with it. Match up the edges all around, and put some pins along the edges to hold the two pieces together. Remember, your pumpkin picture should be on the *inside* of the two pieces of fabric.

5 Thread your needle with yarn. Sew all the way around *three* sides of the pillow. Push the needle from top to bottom and back up to the top to make a running stitch. Remember to leave one side open so that you can turn the pillowcase inside out and stuff the pillow into it!

6 Turn the pillowcase right side out — now your pumpkin painting shows again! Stuff the pillow form or polyester fill into it. Sew up the final side (make sure you tie a knot at the end, so it doesn't pull apart).

Place your pillow on your bed, your favorite chair — or right under your head!

Pumpkin Seed Necklace

WHAT YOU WILL NEED

▶ Pumpkin
▶ Needle and white thread
▶ Paint brushes and poster paint

1 Have someone help you cut open the pumpkin and pull all of the seeds out of it. Wash the seeds and pat them dry. Do *not* let them dry overnight — they should be soft, so that you can poke a needle through them.

2 Thread the needle with the white thread. Push the needle through one of the seeds and pull the thread through the seed until the seed is about 6 inches from the end of the thread. With this tail of thread, tie a good knot around the seed.

3 Push more seeds along the thread. The first seed will keep the others from slipping off.

4 String seeds on the thread until the piece is long enough to go around your neck or wrist. Leave plenty of extra string at this end, too, so that you can tie the two ends together.

5 Dip your brush in paint and carefully paint the seeds — all one color or many different ones. Let the paint dry completely and your jewelry is set to wear!

Make a Musical Instrument

A quick and easy craft project that can be the beginning of a band!

•••WHAT YOU WILL NEED•••

- ◗ 2 aluminum pie plates
- ◗ Many clean pumpkin seeds
- ◗ Stapler
- ◗ Colored stickers and streamers

 3 Decorate the pans with stickers and streamers.

 4 Shake, bang, or shimmy, and listen to what you have created — a seed tambourine!

 1 Fill one pie plate with the pumpkin seeds.

2 Cover this pie plate with the other, so that the insides are facing each other. Staple around the edges. (Use lots of staples so that the pumpkin seeds don't fall out.)

Pumpkin Painting

Plan what kind of pumpkin face you want to make. Is it going to be a baseball player? A fireman? A cowboy? A clown? You decide!

1 Put on an old shirt or smock before you do anything else. *Now* let the fun begin!

2 Place your clean pumpkin on some newspapers. If you can work outside, you won't have to worry about spills!

• • • WHAT YOU WILL NEED • • •

- ▶ Old shirt or painting smock
- ▶ A clean pumpkin
- ▶ Newspaper
- ▶ Poster paints
- ▶ Medium and small paint brushes
- ▶ Extras, such as
     Old cowboy, baseball, fireman, or clown hats
     Shoes or sneakers
     Construction paper and glue

3 Paint everything that will be in one color, let it dry, and then paint everything that will be in the next color. For this clown, paint the big eyes and mouth first, then the pupils and eyelashes, and then fill in the nose and mouth.

4 Add hats, shoes, paper ears . . . whatever!

5 Keep your pumpkin dry so the paint doesn't run. A window, where everyone can see and admire it, is the perfect place!

Make Your Own Fall Foliage Centerpiece

 1 In the center of the table, place your candles about 1 foot apart.

 2 Arrange your pumpkins evenly around the candles. Put the gourds among the pumpkins. Be creative, and see what looks good.

 **3** Tuck your leaves under and around the candles, gourds, and pumpkins. If you don't have enough, grab a few more from outside!

 4 Now, help set the table with plates, glasses, forks, spoons, and knives. Give everyone a napkin. It's your job to count the people, and make sure you have the right number of places.

5 Have someone light the candles, and call everyone to sit down to a beautiful dinner!

Make Your Own Jack-o'-Lantern

••WHAT YOU WILL NEED••

- A large pumpkin
- Warm, soapy water
- Old newspapers
- Crayon and large piece of paper
- Sturdy carving knife
- Sturdy, long-handled spoon
- Pie plate or paper bag for seeds
- Short candles or flashlight
- Funny hat or shoes (optional)

1 Go out to your pumpkin patch and choose your best pumpkin. Wash it with warm, soapy water.

2 Dry your pumpkin completely. A slippery pumpkin is very hard to work with!

3 Spread the newspapers (ones that your parents have already read!) under the pumpkin.

4 Decide on a face — should it be scary? happy? silly? Draw it on a big piece of paper.

5 Get a grown-up to help you carve a circle around the stem to make a lid. The lid should be cut at an angle so that it doesn't fall into the pumpkin. Push and pull with your fingers until the piece comes out.

6 With a big spoon or your hands, pull out the stringy pumpkin goo inside and put it on the newspaper or into a big paper bag. The seeds will be attached to the strings, so don't lose them — you can use them for other projects in this book.

7 When your pumpkin is clean, transfer your drawing to the pumpkin by holding the paper against the pumpkin and poking holes along the lines with a nail or other pointed object. Be sure to poke right into the pumpkin. Let your helper use the "dotted lines" to cut the face just the way you want it.

SOME JACK-O'-LANTERN SAFETY RULES

★ Never use a sharp knife without a grown-up helper!

★ Remind helpers to cut away from themselves!

★ Blow out all candles before you leave the jack-o'-lantern alone or go to sleep!

8 Once the pieces are carved, push and pull them with your fingers to get them out of the pumpkin.

9 Stand back and take a look. It probably looks different than you imagined — that's because the pumpkin is now a jack-o'-lantern, with its own personality!

10 Set your jack-o'-lantern in a safe place, and enjoy its company. If you want to light it, ask an adult to set up a candle inside it.

Try these ideas —

★ Add a baseball cap to your pumpkin, and you've got a "Pittsburgh Pumpkin"!

★ Stack three small pumpkins by your door and carve a face for the top one. You'll have an early, orange snowman!

★ Stack pumpkins with different faces on top of each other for a pumpkin totem pole!

★ Instead of a pumpkin lid, use a turban-style squash as a "hat" for your pumpkin.

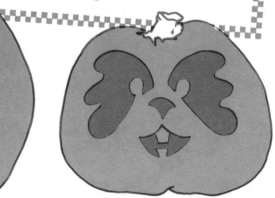

Pumpkin Lore

Jack of the Lantern

In the 1800s, Irish immigrants to America brought this story about Jack of the Lantern. The legend says that Jack was a greedy man, so stingy he couldn't get into Heaven. And, he played so many tricks on people that the Devil wouldn't take him either! So, Jack was forced to walk around until Judgment Day looking for a resting place. He stuffed a lighted piece of coal into a turnip to use as a lantern to see by. As the years went by, Americans began using a pumpkin instead of a turnip for Jack's lantern — and now we have Jack-o'-Lanterns to light our way!

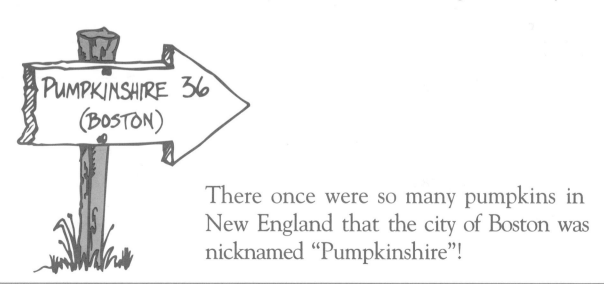

There once were so many pumpkins in New England that the city of Boston was nicknamed "Pumpkinshire"!

Puzzling Pumpkins!

How many different words can you make by using the letters in the words **PUMPKIN PATCH?** See what your record is!

1._____

2._____

3._____

4._____

5._____

6._____

7._____

8._____

9._____

10._____

11._____

12._____

13._____

14._____

15._____

16._____

17._____

18._____

19._____

20._____

21._____

22._____

23._____

24._____

25._____

26._____

27._____

28._____

29._____

30._____

31._____

32._____

33._____

34._____

35._____

36._____

37._____

38._____

39._____

PART III

Be a Pumpkin Cook

Good — and good *for* you, too? That is true of the snacks you can create as you mix and stir pumpkin in the tasty recipes that follow. Pumpkin pie is the old favorite, but wouldn't the Pilgrims have been excited to see Maple Pumpkin Cookies on the Thanksgiving menu!

Grab a grown-up helper by the hand and head for the kitchen! A pair of clean hands, mixing tools, and a hot oven are all you need to create lots of tempting treats.

*(One 15-ounce can of pumpkin contains a little less than
2 cups of cooked, mashed pumpkin.)*

THE FIRST PUMPKIN PIE

The Pilgrims invented pumpkin pie. They baked the pumpkin in the ashes of a fire. When it was cooked, they removed the top and added honey and maple syrup to the warm pumpkin inside. Mmm-mmm, *good!*

Good Kitchen Tips

★ Always wash your hands before working with food.

★ Have an adult helper with you when you work in the kitchen.

★ Read carefully! Look over the entire recipe before starting, so you know that you have all the ingredients and cooking equipment that you need.

★ Try not to waste food. Measure carefully and use just what you need.

★ Be helpful. Do as much as you can to help with the project you choose.

★ Clean up! A messy kitchen is not fun to work in. It's easier if you clean up as you go along!

Pumpkin Soup

WHAT YOU WILL NEED

- 2 tablespoons butter
- ½ cup chopped onion
- 4 cups chicken stock
- ¼ teaspoon ground ginger
- ¼ teaspoon ground nutmeg
- 3 cups cooked pumpkin pulp
- Corn chips

1 In a soup pot, melt the butter over medium heat on top of the stove. Sauté the onion in it for 5 minutes.

2 Add the stock, ginger, nutmeg, and pumpkin. Bring the mixture to a boil.

3 Turn the heat down to low, and simmer the soup for 10 minutes until it is thick. Stir it every so often so that it doesn't stick to the pan and burn. Serve in a Pumpkin Tureen. (*See next page.*)

35

Pumpkin Tureen

A tureen is a big pot from which soup is served. You're going to make a tureen from a real pumpkin!

1 Wash and dry your pumpkin. (Do not use Bleach Solution to wash this pumpkin.)

2 Draw a lid on your pumpkin. Be sure to make the opening big enough for your ladle.

3 Ask a grown-up helper to cut the lid away. Make the cut on an angle so that the lid won't fall into the pumpkin. Pull out lid in one piece.

4 Scrape the inside clean with a big spoon. Be careful not to break the flesh (the sides of the pumpkin). You don't want a leaky pumpkin pot!

5 Fill the tureen with soup. Serve it with a smile, where everyone can see your creation. Ladle the soup into bowls, and sprinkle corn chips on top.

The Pilgrims used pumpkins for lots of different purposes. They dried pumpkins and made the shells into bowls for eating, as well as jars where they could keep their grains and seeds. They used the cooked purée for pies and breads. And, they dried the seeds to eat — these were an energy food, packed with vitamins.

Fried Pumpkin Flowers

Try this for a special and unusual treat! Be sure to have adult help — hot oil can be dangerous to work with.

1 Wash the flowers and dry them with a paper towel.

•••WHAT YOU WILL NEED•••

- 15-20 pumpkin blossoms (remember, when you pick a blossom, no pumpkin will grow there!)
- ½ cup whole wheat flour
- 1 tablespoon safflower oil
- ⅛ teaspoon salt
- ¼ teaspoon baking powder
- ¼ teaspoon ground nutmeg
- 1 cup beer
- ½ cup milk
- Additional safflower oil for frying
- Additional salt

2 Blend the flour, oil, salt, baking powder, nutmeg, beer, and milk to make a batter, and beat it with a wooden spoon until it is smooth.

3 Place a few tablespoons of safflower oil in a pan. Use just enough oil to coat the bottom of the pan.

4 Dip the flowers into the batter. Let any extra batter drip back into the bowl before you fry the flowers in the hot oil. Turn each flower only once, and cook them just until they are crispy. Cook only a few flowers at a time — they need plenty of room to cook nicely. Add more oil if the pan starts to get dry.

5 Drain the flowers on paper towel. Sprinkle them with salt, and eat!

Pumpkin Waffles

Start your day with some fun!

• • • WHAT YOU WILL NEED • • •

- ▶ 2 cups flour
- ▶ 2 teaspoons baking powder
- ▶ ¼ teaspoon ground cinnamon
- ▶ ¼ teaspoon ground ginger
- ▶ ¼ teaspoon ground nutmeg
- ▶ ½ teaspoon salt
- ▶ 3 beaten eggs
- ▶ 1¾ cups milk
- ▶ ¾ cup mashed pumpkin
- ▶ ½ cup cooking oil
- ▶ ½ cup chopped nuts

 1 In a large bowl, mix together the flour, baking powder, cinnamon, ginger, nutmeg, and salt.

 2 In another bowl, mix the eggs, milk, pumpkin, and cooking oil.

 3 Combine the egg mixture with the flour mixture.

 4 Stir in the nuts. Mix the whole thing well.

 5 Cook the batter in a hot waffle iron. Serve with butter and maple syrup or honey!

Pumpkins Afloat!

Toss your pumpkin carefully into a tub or pool full of water, and watch it roll around on its back.

In colonial times, there once was a pumpkin flood. It rained so much and so hard that pumpkin fields were flooded and thousands of pumpkins floated into the villages!

Pumpkin Snack Chips

You will need adult help to slice and deep-fry your chips.

···WHAT YOU WILL NEED···

- A small pumpkin (about ½ pound)
- Bowl of ice water
- Oil for deep-fat frying
- ½ teaspoon garlic salt
- 1½ tablespoons curry powder

1 Peel the pumpkin, cut it in half, and remove the seeds.

2 Cut the pumpkin flesh into 2-inch strips, and then use a grater to slice the strips as thinly as possible into potato-chip-size pieces.

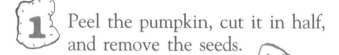

3 Put the chips into a bowl of ice water, and chill in the refrigerator for 45 minutes.

4 Drain off the water. Pat the chips dry with a paper towel.

5 Deep-fry the chips until they are browned.

6 Sprinkle them with garlic salt and curry powder. Pack these in with your sandwich to munch with lunch!

DID YOU KNOW —

There is a sunfish called a *pumpkinseed* fish! Small and very brightly colored, pumpkinseeds live in freshwater ponds and lakes in North America. Their scientific name is *Lepomis gibbosus*.

Joey's Lunch

Milk

Pumpkin Pie

Makes two 8-inch pies

...WHAT YOU WILL NEED...

For the Crust

- 3 cups gingersnap crumbs
- 2 tablespoons honey
- 8 tablespoons melted butter
- 1 cup chopped nuts
- 1 teaspoon cinnamon

For the Filling

- 2½ cups mashed, cooked pumpkin
- Two 15-ounce cans of condensed milk
- 4 eggs
- ½ teaspoon salt
- 1 teaspoon ground ginger
- 1 teaspoon ground nutmeg
- 2 teaspoons ground cinnamon
- ¼ teaspoon ground cloves
- 1 cup brown sugar, packed
- Whipped cream (optional)

1 Preheat the oven to 375°F.

2 To make the gingersnap crumbs, put a few gingersnaps at a time into a paper bag and twist the bag closed. Roll over the bag with a rolling pin, pressing hard to crush the cookies.

3 Put the crumbs and the rest of the crust ingredients in a big bowl. Mix them well — it's easy and fun to mix them with your fingers.

4 Divide the crust mixture between two 8-inch pie plates. Use your fingers to spread it evenly on the bottom and sides of the plates. Press it firmly against the plates.

5 In a large bowl, mix all the Filling ingredients except the whipped cream. Beat the mixture with a spoon until it's completely smooth.

6 Pour the mixture into your pie shells. Bake in the preheated oven for 50-55 minutes. When you think the pies are done, stick a knife carefully into the middle of one. If it comes out clean, without any pie sticking to it, the pie is ready to take out of the oven.

7 Serve your pie at room temperature or cold. Whipped cream always tastes good on top!

Pumpkin Rolls

Makes 2 dozen rolls

•••WHAT YOU WILL NEED•••

- 1 cup milk
- ¼ cup maple syrup
- 4 tablespoons butter
- 2 teaspoons salt
- 1 cup cooked pumpkin, drained and mashed
- 1½ tablespoons dry yeast
- ¼ cup warm water
- ½ teaspoon honey
- 2 eggs
- 1 teaspoon grated orange peel
- 6½ cups flour (approximately)
- Melted butter to brush on rolls

1 In a saucepan, heat the milk until bubbles appear around the edge (this is called *scalding*). Stir in the maple syrup, butter, salt, and pumpkin. Mix well. Take the pan off the stove and let the mixture sit until it is lukewarm.

2 In a large bowl, dissolve the yeast in the warm water with the honey. When it is bubbly, add the cooled milk-pumpkin mixture, eggs, orange peel, and 2½ cups of the flour.

Beat this mixture with an electric mixer for 2 minutes *or* beat the mixture with a wooden spoon for at least 200 strokes. This gets tiring, so you might want to take turns with someone else.

3 Gradually add more flour until the dough pulls away from the side of the bowl and gets stiff enough to form into a ball that you can knead and squeeze with your hands.

After awhile, the dough will start to get less sticky, smoother, and more elastic. When dough is elastic, you can poke your finger into it and the dough will spring back. This means you can stop kneading.

4 It's time to knead the dough! Put flour on your hands and flour on the counter where you are working. Put the dough on the counter, and turn it over and over until it is coated with flour.

Pull some of the dough from the back of the ball over to the front, as though you were folding a piece of paper. Press down on the folded dough and push the ball away from you. Turn the ball of dough a little bit, and fold it and push it again. Do this over and over. You can sprinkle more flour on the counter and on your hands to keep things from sticking too much.

5 Spread butter all over the inside of a mixing bowl. Put the ball of dough into the bowl. Turn the dough over, so that the top is

coated with some of the butter from the bowl. Cover the bowl with a piece of plastic wrap and put it in a nice warm place. Notice how large the ball of dough is. In about 1 hour, the yeast will make it "rise" until it is about twice as big as it is now — this is called "doubling."

 6 When the dough is doubled, make a fist and gently punch right down in the middle of the dough. Put the dough on a floured counter, and knead it a few times. Cut the dough into pieces about the size of eggs. Cover the "eggs" and let them rest for 10 or 15 minutes.

7 Spread butter in muffin tins. Place the egg-shaped rolls into the muffin tins. Brush the tops of the rolls with some melted butter. Cover them with plastic wrap, and let them rise again for about ½ hour — not quite until doubled this time. Preheat the oven to 375°F while they are rising.

8 Bake the rolls in the pre-heated oven for 15 minutes. Eat them while they are still warm!

A Bonny Bowl

Did you ever think of using your pumpkin shell as a cereal bowl? Here's an old English nursery rhyme that tells about doing that. In this poem, "bonny" means "good-looking and excellent."

Little lad, little lad, where wast
thou born?

Far off in Lancashire, under a
thorn,

Where they sup buttermilk from a
ram's horn,

And a pumpkin scooped, with a
yellow rim,

Is the bonny bowl they breakfast in.

Raisin-Pumpkin Cookies

Makes 4 dozen cookies

•••WHAT YOU WILL NEED•••

- 2½ cups flour
- ½ teaspoon salt
- ½ teaspoon baking soda
- ½ teaspoon ground nutmeg
- ¼ teaspoon ground cinnamon
- ¼ teaspoon ground ginger
- ½ teaspoon vanilla extract
- ¾ cup cooking oil
- 1 egg
- 1¼ cups brown sugar
- 1 cup mashed, cooked pumpkin
- 2 cups raisins

 Preheat oven to 350°F. Butter a cookie sheet.

 In a large bowl, sift together the flour, salt, baking soda, nutmeg, cinnamon, and ginger.

 In another bowl, combine the vanilla, oil, egg, brown sugar, and pumpkin. Beat well with a wooden spoon.

 Add the flour mixture and the raisins to the pumpkin mixture. Stir well.

5 Drop spoonfuls of batter onto the buttered cookie sheet. Don't put cookies too close together, because they spread out when they are cooking.

 6 Bake the cookies in the preheated oven for 20 minutes or until they are lightly browned. Let them set on the cookie sheet for about 2 minutes after taking them from the oven, and then place them on a rack to cool.

 7 Pour a big glass of milk, and enjoy!

Hand a Raisin-Pumpkin Cookie to your school bus driver — she'll hum all the way home!

Maple-Pumpkin Cookies

Make these and take them to school for a class treat!

Makes 3 dozen cookies

····WHAT YOU WILL NEED····

- 1 cup mashed, cooked pumpkin
- 1 cup maple syrup
- 1 egg
- 1 teaspoon vanilla extract
- ½ cup unsalted butter
- 1 cup whole wheat flour
- 1 cup all-purpose flour
- 1 teaspoon baking soda
- 1 teaspoon baking powder
- ½ teaspoon ground cinnamon
- ½ teaspoon ground nutmeg
- ½ teaspoon salt
- ½ cup chopped pecans
- 1 cup grated apple

 Preheat the oven to 350°F. Grease a cookie sheet.

 Combine the pumpkin, maple syrup, egg, and vanilla in a blender. Mix until smooth.

 With an electric mixer, cream the butter in a small bowl. Add the creamed butter to the pumpkin mixture.

 In another bowl, mix the flours, baking soda, baking powder, cinnamon, nutmeg, and salt. Add half of this to the pumpkin mixture, and mix well. Add the rest, and again mix well. Gently stir in the nuts and apples.

5 Spoon the dough onto the greased cookie sheet, leaving plenty of room for the cookies to spread. Bake them for 15-20 minutes or until they are lightly brown on the edges.

Curl up with a plate of cookies, a glass of cider, and a book of scarey Halloween stories or Charles Schultz's *It's the Great Pumpkin, Charlie Brown!*

Pumpkin Seeds

WHAT YOU WILL NEED

▸ Pumpkin seeds (about 2 cups)
▸ Paper towel
▸ 1 tablespoon cooking oil
▸ Cookie sheet or frying pan
▸ Salt, to taste

Pumpkin seeds are always a good addition to salads, breads, or muffins, or just to eat for a snack. Good *for* you — and *good* to eat!

Whenever you clean out a pumpkin, remove the seeds from the pumpkin goo and wash them thoroughly. Let them dry for a day or so on a paper towel. Then, roast them or fry them, and sprinkle them with salt for a pumpkin seed snack.

To roast your seeds —

Put 1 tablespoon of oil in a bowl, add the dried seeds, and toss them until they are all coated with oil. Spread them out on a cookie sheet. Bake them in a 350°F oven for about ½ to 1 hour. Stir them every 10 or 15 minutes while they are baking.

To fry your seeds —

Put 1 tablespoon of oil in a frying pan. Add the dried seeds, and cook over Medium/High heat on top of the stove. When they begin to swell and pop a bit, take them off the heat. Keep the top of the pan handy while you're cooking — a few might try to escape!

Pumpkin seeds have been used since ancient times as a source of protein, minerals, and vitamins.

Pumpkin Bread

Makes two loaves

···**WHAT YOU WILL NEED**···

- 3 cups mashed, cooked pumpkin
- 1 cup safflower oil
- 1 cup honey
- 1 cup yogurt
- 2 eggs
- 1 teaspoon salt
- 1 teaspoon ground cinnamon
- 1 teaspoon ground cloves
- 4 teaspoons baking soda
- 4 cups whole wheat flour

1 Preheat the oven to 325°F. Oil two 4½" x 8½" bread pans.

2 Put all the ingredients except the flour into a big bowl. Mix well.

3 Add the flour, a little at a time. Stir well.

4 Taste your batter, and if it doesn't seem sweet enough for you, add a bit more honey.

5 Spoon the batter into the prepared bread pans, and bake the bread in the preheated oven for about 1 hour. To see if the bread is done, stick a wire tester into the center. If the wire comes out perfectly clean, the bread is done.

6 Cool the breads in the pans on a rack. To serve, spread slices with Pumpkin Butter, cream cheese, or apple butter for a sweet treat!

Pumpkin Butter

- 1 cup of mashed, cooked pumpkin
- ½ cup honey
- ¼ cup molasses
- 1 tablespoon lemon juice
- ¾ teaspoon ground cinnamon

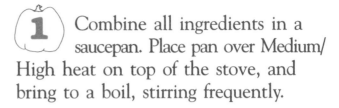 **1** Combine all ingredients in a saucepan. Place pan over Medium/High heat on top of the stove, and bring to a boil, stirring frequently.

2 Turn the heat down to low, and simmer until the mixture is thick, about 15 minutes. Be sure to stir it often, as it burns easily.

3 Cool, then chill for at least 1 hour before using, or freeze.

Crossword Puzzle

1. <u>P</u> __ __ __ __ __

2. __ __ <u>U</u> __ __ __

3. <u>M</u> __ __ __ __ __

4. <u>P</u> __ __ __ __ __

5. __ __ __ <u>K</u> __ __ __ __ __ __ __ __

6. __ <u>I</u> __

7. __ __ __ __ __ <u>N</u> __

Clues going across:

1. Where a pumpkin grows.

2. You can make your pumpkin _____ by making it grow within a milk carton.

3. It takes about 4 _____ for a pumpkin to grow.

4. If your pumpkin is the best, it might win a _____!

5. What you carve at Halloween.

6. A yummy dessert recipe, first created by the Pilgrims, pumpkin _____.

7. The Pilgrims and the _____ planted lots of pumpkins.